VEHICLE INFORMATION

ake: ______________________________

ear: ______________ License Plate: ______________

N: ______________________________

urchase Date: ______________ From: ______________

ealer Info: ______________________________

egistration: ______________________________

____

surance Company: ______________________________

gent: ______________________________

hone: ______________________________

licy: ______________________________

otes: ______________________________

____

____

Date/Time	Oil Changed	Rotate/Balance Tires	Tire Replaced	Wheel Alignment	Air Filter	Fuel Filter	Brakes Serviced	Spark Plugs	Transmission	Wiper Blades	Batteries	Radiator	Belts & Hoses	Mileage

OTHER MAINTENANCE / REPAIRS LOG

Date/Time	Description	Mileage

Date/Time	Oil Changed	Rotate/Balance Tires	Tire Replaced	Wheel Alignment	Air Filter	Fuel Filter	Brakes Serviced	Spark Plugs	Transmission	Wiper Blades	Batteries	Radiator	Belts & Hoses	Mileage

OTHER MAINTENANCE / REPAIRS LOG

Date/Time	Description	Mileage

Date/Time	Oil Changed	Rotate/Balance Tires	Tire Replaced	Wheel Alignment	Air Filter	Fuel Filter	Brakes Serviced	Spark Plugs	Transmission	Wiper Blades	Batteries	Radiator	Belts & Hoses	Mileage

OTHER MAINTENANCE / REPAIRS LOG

Date/Time	Description	Mileage

Date/Time	Oil Changed	Rotate/Balance Tires	Tire Replaced	Wheel Alignment	Air Filter	Fuel Filter	Brakes Serviced	Spark Plugs	Transmission	Wiper Blades	Batteries	Radiator	Belts & Hoses	Mileage

OTHER MAINTENANCE / REPAIRS LOG

Date/Time	Description	Mileage

Date/Time	Oil Changed	Rotate/Balance Tires	Tire Replaced	Wheel Alignment	Air Filter	Fuel Filter	Brakes Serviced	Spark Plugs	Transmission	Wiper Blades	Batteries	Radiator	Belts & Hoses	Mileage

OTHER MAINTENANCE / REPAIRS LOG

Date/Time	Description	Mileage

Date/Time	Oil Changed	Rotate/Balance Tires	Tire Replaced	Wheel Alignment	Air Filter	Fuel Filter	Brakes Serviced	Spark Plugs	Transmission	Wiper Blades	Batteries	Radiator	Belts & Hoses	Mileage

OTHER MAINTENANCE / REPAIRS LOG

Date/Time	Description	Mileage

Date/Time	Oil Changed	Rotate/Balance Tires	Tire Replaced	Wheel Alignment	Air Filter	Fuel Filter	Brakes Serviced	Spark Plugs	Transmission	Wiper Blades	Batteries	Radiator	Belts & Hoses	Mileage

OTHER MAINTENANCE / REPAIRS LOG

Date/Time	Description	Mileage

Date/Time	Oil Changed	Rotate/Balance Tires	Tire Replaced	Wheel Alignment	Air Filter	Fuel Filter	Brakes Serviced	Spark Plugs	Transmission	Wiper Blades	Batteries	Radiator	Belts & Hoses	Mileage

OTHER MAINTENANCE / REPAIRS LOG

Date/Time	Description	Mileage

Date/Time	Oil Changed	Rotate/Balance Tires	Tire Replaced	Wheel Alignment	Air Filter	Fuel Filter	Brakes Serviced	Spark Plugs	Transmission	Wiper Blades	Batteries	Radiator	Belts & Hoses	Mileage

OTHER MAINTENANCE / REPAIRS LOG

Date/Time	Description	Mileage

Date/Time	Oil Changed	Rotate/Balance Tires	Tire Replaced	Wheel Alignment	Air Filter	Fuel Filter	Brakes Serviced	Spark Plugs	Transmission	Wiper Blades	Batteries	Radiator	Belts & Hoses	Mileage

OTHER MAINTENANCE / REPAIRS LOG

Date/Time	Description	Mileage

Date/Time	Oil Changed	Rotate/Balance Tires	Tire Replaced	Wheel Alignment	Air Filter	Fuel Filter	Brakes Serviced	Spark Plugs	Transmission	Wiper Blades	Batteries	Radiator	Belts & Hoses	Mileage

OTHER MAINTENANCE / REPAIRS LOG

Date/Time	Description	Mileage

Date/Time	Oil Changed	Rotate/Balance Tires	Tire Replaced	Wheel Alignment	Air Filter	Fuel Filter	Brakes Serviced	Spark Plugs	Transmission	Wiper Blades	Batteries	Radiator	Belts & Hoses	Mileage

OTHER MAINTENANCE / REPAIRS LOG

Date/Time	Description	Mileage

Date/Time	Oil Changed	Rotate/Balance Tires	Tire Replaced	Wheel Alignment	Air Filter	Fuel Filter	Brakes Serviced	Spark Plugs	Transmission	Wiper Blades	Batteries	Radiator	Belts & Hoses	Mileage

OTHER MAINTENANCE / REPAIRS LOG

Date/Time	Description	Mileage

Date/Time	Oil Changed	Rotate/Balance Tires	Tire Replaced	Wheel Alignment	Air Filter	Fuel Filter	Brakes Serviced	Spark Plugs	Transmission	Wiper Blades	Batteries	Radiator	Belts & Hoses	Mileage

OTHER MAINTENANCE / REPAIRS LOG

Date/Time	Description	Mileage

Date/Time	Oil Changed	Rotate/Balance Tires	Tire Replaced	Wheel Alignment	Air Filter	Fuel Filter	Brakes Serviced	Spark Plugs	Transmission	Wiper Blades	Batteries	Radiator	Belts & Hoses	Mileage

OTHER MAINTENANCE / REPAIRS LOG

Date/Time	Description	Mileage

Date/Time	Oil Changed	Rotate/Balance Tires	Tire Replaced	Wheel Alignment	Air Filter	Fuel Filter	Brakes Serviced	Spark Plugs	Transmission	Wiper Blades	Batteries	Radiator	Belts & Hoses	Mileage

OTHER MAINTENANCE / REPAIRS LOG

Date/Time	Description	Mileage

Date/Time	Oil Changed	Rotate/Balance Tires	Tire Replaced	Wheel Alignment	Air Filter	Fuel Filter	Brakes Serviced	Spark Plugs	Transmission	Wiper Blades	Batteries	Radiator	Belts & Hoses	Mileage

OTHER MAINTENANCE / REPAIRS LOG

Date/Time	Description	Mileage

Date/Time	Oil Changed	Rotate/Balance Tires	Tire Replaced	Wheel Alignment	Air Filter	Fuel Filter	Brakes Serviced	Spark Plugs	Transmission	Wiper Blades	Batteries	Radiator	Belts & Hoses	Mileage

OTHER MAINTENANCE / REPAIRS LOG

Date/Time	Description	Mileage

Date/Time	Oil Changed	Rotate/Balance Tires	Tire Replaced	Wheel Alignment	Air Filter	Fuel Filter	Brakes Serviced	Spark Plugs	Transmission	Wiper Blades	Batteries	Radiator	Belts & Hoses	Mileage

OTHER MAINTENANCE / REPAIRS LOG

Date/Time	Description	Mileage

Date/Time	Oil Changed	Rotate/Balance Tires	Tire Replaced	Wheel Alignment	Air Filter	Fuel Filter	Brakes Serviced	Spark Plugs	Transmission	Wiper Blades	Batteries	Radiator	Belts & Hoses	Mileage

OTHER MAINTENANCE / REPAIRS LOG

Date/Time	Description	Mileage

Date/Time	Oil Changed	Rotate/Balance Tires	Tire Replaced	Wheel Alignment	Air Filter	Fuel Filter	Brakes Serviced	Spark Plugs	Transmission	Wiper Blades	Batteries	Radiator	Belts & Hoses	Mileage

OTHER MAINTENANCE / REPAIRS LOG

Date/Time	Description	Mileage

Date/Time	Oil Changed	Rotate/Balance Tires	Tire Replaced	Wheel Alignment	Air Filter	Fuel Filter	Brakes Serviced	Spark Plugs	Transmission	Wiper Blades	Batteries	Radiator	Belts & Hoses	Mileage

OTHER MAINTENANCE / REPAIRS LOG

Date/Time	Description	Mileage

Date/Time	Oil Changed	Rotate/Balance Tires	Tire Replaced	Wheel Alignment	Air Filter	Fuel Filter	Brakes Serviced	Spark Plugs	Transmission	Wiper Blades	Batteries	Radiator	Belts & Hoses	Mileage

OTHER MAINTENANCE / REPAIRS LOG

Date/Time	Description	Mileage

Date/Time	Oil Changed	Rotate/Balance Tires	Tire Replaced	Wheel Alignment	Air Filter	Fuel Filter	Brakes Serviced	Spark Plugs	Transmission	Wiper Blades	Batteries	Radiator	Belts & Hoses	Mileage

OTHER MAINTENANCE / REPAIRS LOG

Date/Time	Description	Mileage

Date/Time	Oil Changed	Rotate/Balance Tires	Tire Replaced	Wheel Alignment	Air Filter	Fuel Filter	Brakes Serviced	Spark Plugs	Transmission	Wiper Blades	Batteries	Radiator	Belts & Hoses	Mileage

OTHER MAINTENANCE / REPAIRS LOG

Date/Time	Description	Mileage

Date/Time	Oil Changed	Rotate/Balance Tires	Tire Replaced	Wheel Alignment	Air Filter	Fuel Filter	Brakes Serviced	Spark Plugs	Transmission	Wiper Blades	Batteries	Radiator	Belts & Hoses	Mileage

OTHER MAINTENANCE / REPAIRS LOG

Date/Time	Description	Mileage

Date/Time	Oil Changed	Rotate/Balance Tires	Tire Replaced	Wheel Alignment	Air Filter	Fuel Filter	Brakes Serviced	Spark Plugs	Transmission	Wiper Blades	Batteries	Radiator	Belts & Hoses	Mileage

OTHER MAINTENANCE / REPAIRS LOG

Date/Time	Description	Mileage

Date/Time	Oil Changed	Rotate/Balance Tires	Tire Replaced	Wheel Alignment	Air Filter	Fuel Filter	Brakes Serviced	Spark Plugs	Transmission	Wiper Blades	Batteries	Radiator	Belts & Hoses	Mileage

OTHER MAINTENANCE / REPAIRS LOG

Date/Time	Description	Mileage

Date/Time	Oil Changed	Rotate/Balance Tires	Tire Replaced	Wheel Alignment	Air Filter	Fuel Filter	Brakes Serviced	Spark Plugs	Transmission	Wiper Blades	Batteries	Radiator	Belts & Hoses	Mileage

OTHER MAINTENANCE / REPAIRS LOG

Date/Time	Description	Mileage

Date/Time	Oil Changed	Rotate/Balance Tires	Tire Replaced	Wheel Alignment	Air Filter	Fuel Filter	Brakes Serviced	Spark Plugs	Transmission	Wiper Blades	Batteries	Radiator	Belts & Hoses	Mileage

OTHER MAINTENANCE / REPAIRS LOG

Date/Time	Description	Mileage

Date/Time	Oil Changed	Rotate/Balance Tires	Tire Replaced	Wheel Alignment	Air Filter	Fuel Filter	Brakes Serviced	Spark Plugs	Transmission	Wiper Blades	Batteries	Radiator	Belts & Hoses	Mileage

OTHER MAINTENANCE / REPAIRS LOG

Date/Time	Description	Mileage

Date/Time	Oil Changed	Rotate/Balance Tires	Tire Replaced	Wheel Alignment	Air Filter	Fuel Filter	Brakes Serviced	Spark Plugs	Transmission	Wiper Blades	Batteries	Radiator	Belts & Hoses	Mileage

OTHER MAINTENANCE / REPAIRS LOG

Date/Time	Description	Mileage

Date/Time	Oil Changed	Rotate/Balance Tires	Tire Replaced	Wheel Alignment	Air Filter	Fuel Filter	Brakes Serviced	Spark Plugs	Transmission	Wiper Blades	Batteries	Radiator	Belts & Hoses	Mileage

OTHER MAINTENANCE / REPAIRS LOG

Date/Time	Description	Mileage

Date/Time	Oil Changed	Rotate/Balance Tires	Tire Replaced	Wheel Alignment	Air Filter	Fuel Filter	Brakes Serviced	Spark Plugs	Transmission	Wiper Blades	Batteries	Radiator	Belts & Hoses	Mileage

OTHER MAINTENANCE / REPAIRS LOG

Date/Time	Description	Mileage

Date/Time	Oil Changed	Rotate/Balance Tires	Tire Replaced	Wheel Alignment	Air Filter	Fuel Filter	Brakes Serviced	Spark Plugs	Transmission	Wiper Blades	Batteries	Radiator	Belts & Hoses	Mileage

OTHER MAINTENANCE / REPAIRS LOG

Date/Time	Description	Mileage

Date/Time	Oil Changed	Rotate/Balance Tires	Tire Replaced	Wheel Alignment	Air Filter	Fuel Filter	Brakes Serviced	Spark Plugs	Transmission	Wiper Blades	Batteries	Radiator	Belts & Hoses	Mileage

OTHER MAINTENANCE / REPAIRS LOG

Date/Time	Description	Mileage

Date/Time	Oil Changed	Rotate/Balance Tires	Tire Replaced	Wheel Alignment	Air Filter	Fuel Filter	Brakes Serviced	Spark Plugs	Transmission	Wiper Blades	Batteries	Radiator	Belts & Hoses	Mileage

OTHER MAINTENANCE / REPAIRS LOG

Date/Time	Description	Mileage

Date/Time	Oil Changed	Rotate/Balance Tires	Tire Replaced	Wheel Alignment	Air Filter	Fuel Filter	Brakes Serviced	Spark Plugs	Transmission	Wiper Blades	Batteries	Radiator	Belts & Hoses	Mileage

OTHER MAINTENANCE / REPAIRS LOG

Date/Time	Description	Mileage

Date/Time	Oil Changed	Rotate/Balance Tires	Tire Replaced	Wheel Alignment	Air Filter	Fuel Filter	Brakes Serviced	Spark Plugs	Transmission	Wiper Blades	Batteries	Radiator	Belts & Hoses	Mileage

OTHER MAINTENANCE / REPAIRS LOG

Date/Time	Description	Mileage

Date/Time	Oil Changed	Rotate/Balance Tires	Tire Replaced	Wheel Alignment	Air Filter	Fuel Filter	Brakes Serviced	Spark Plugs	Transmission	Wiper Blades	Batteries	Radiator	Belts & Hoses	Mileage

OTHER MAINTENANCE / REPAIRS LOG

Date/Time	Description	Mileage

Date/Time	Oil Changed	Rotate/Balance Tires	Tire Replaced	Wheel Alignment	Air Filter	Fuel Filter	Brakes Serviced	Spark Plugs	Transmission	Wiper Blades	Batteries	Radiator	Belts & Hoses	Mileage

OTHER MAINTENANCE / REPAIRS LOG

Date/Time	Description	Mileage

Date/Time	Oil Changed	Rotate/Balance Tires	Tire Replaced	Wheel Alignment	Air Filter	Fuel Filter	Brakes Serviced	Spark Plugs	Transmission	Wiper Blades	Batteries	Radiator	Belts & Hoses	Mileage

OTHER MAINTENANCE / REPAIRS LOG

Date/Time	Description	Mileage

Date/Time	Oil Changed	Rotate/Balance Tires	Tire Replaced	Wheel Alignment	Air Filter	Fuel Filter	Brakes Serviced	Spark Plugs	Transmission	Wiper Blades	Batteries	Radiator	Belts & Hoses	Mileage

OTHER MAINTENANCE / REPAIRS LOG

Date/Time	Description	Mileage

Date/Time	Oil Changed	Rotate/Balance Tires	Tire Replaced	Wheel Alignment	Air Filter	Fuel Filter	Brakes Serviced	Spark Plugs	Transmission	Wiper Blades	Batteries	Radiator	Belts & Hoses	Mileage

OTHER MAINTENANCE / REPAIRS LOG

Date/Time	Description	Mileage

Date/Time	Oil Changed	Rotate/Balance Tires	Tire Replaced	Wheel Alignment	Air Filter	Fuel Filter	Brakes Serviced	Spark Plugs	Transmission	Wiper Blades	Batteries	Radiator	Belts & Hoses	Mileage

OTHER MAINTENANCE / REPAIRS LOG

Date/Time	Description	Mileage

Date/Time	Oil Changed	Rotate/Balance Tires	Tire Replaced	Wheel Alignment	Air Filter	Fuel Filter	Brakes Serviced	Spark Plugs	Transmission	Wiper Blades	Batteries	Radiator	Belts & Hoses	Mileage

OTHER MAINTENANCE / REPAIRS LOG

Date/Time	Description	Mileage

Date/Time	Oil Changed	Rotate/Balance Tires	Tire Replaced	Wheel Alignment	Air Filter	Fuel Filter	Brakes Serviced	Spark Plugs	Transmission	Wiper Blades	Batteries	Radiator	Belts & Hoses	Mileage

OTHER MAINTENANCE / REPAIRS LOG

Date/Time	Description	Mileage

Date/Time	Oil Changed	Rotate/Balance Tires	Tire Replaced	Wheel Alignment	Air Filter	Fuel Filter	Brakes Serviced	Spark Plugs	Transmission	Wiper Blades	Batteries	Radiator	Belts & Hoses	Mileage

OTHER MAINTENANCE / REPAIRS LOG

Date/Time	Description	Mileage

Date/Time	Oil Changed	Rotate/Balance Tires	Tire Replaced	Wheel Alignment	Air Filter	Fuel Filter	Brakes Serviced	Spark Plugs	Transmission	Wiper Blades	Batteries	Radiator	Belts & Hoses	Mileage

OTHER MAINTENANCE / REPAIRS LOG

Date/Time	Description	Mileage

Date/Time	Oil Changed	Rotate/Balance Tires	Tire Replaced	Wheel Alignment	Air Filter	Fuel Filter	Brakes Serviced	Spark Plugs	Transmission	Wiper Blades	Batteries	Radiator	Belts & Hoses	Mileage

OTHER MAINTENANCE / REPAIRS LOG

Date/Time	Description	Mileage

Date/Time	Oil Changed	Rotate/Balance Tires	Tire Replaced	Wheel Alignment	Air Filter	Fuel Filter	Brakes Serviced	Spark Plugs	Transmission	Wiper Blades	Batteries	Radiator	Belts & Hoses	Mileage

OTHER MAINTENANCE / REPAIRS LOG

Date/Time	Description	Mileage

Date/Time	Oil Changed	Rotate/Balance Tires	Tire Replaced	Wheel Alignment	Air Filter	Fuel Filter	Brakes Serviced	Spark Plugs	Transmission	Wiper Blades	Batteries	Radiator	Belts & Hoses	Mileage

OTHER MAINTENANCE / REPAIRS LOG

Date/Time	Description	Mileage

Date/Time	Oil Changed	Rotate/Balance Tires	Tire Replaced	Wheel Alignment	Air Filter	Fuel Filter	Brakes Serviced	Spark Plugs	Transmission	Wiper Blades	Batteries	Radiator	Belts & Hoses	Mileage

OTHER MAINTENANCE / REPAIRS LOG

Date/Time	Description	Mileage

Date/Time	Oil Changed	Rotate/Balance Tires	Tire Replaced	Wheel Alignment	Air Filter	Fuel Filter	Brakes Serviced	Spark Plugs	Transmission	Wiper Blades	Batteries	Radiator	Belts & Hoses	Mileage

OTHER MAINTENANCE / REPAIRS LOG

Date/Time	Description	Mileage

Made in United States
Troutdale, OR
10/20/2023

13862221R00066